PERSONAL FREEDOM & CIVIC DUTY ™

UNDERSTANDING YOUR
RIGHTS IN THE
INFORMATION AGE

SUZANNE WEINICK

ROSEN
PUBLISHING®

New York

Published in 2014 by The Rosen Publishing Group, Inc.
29 East 21st Street, New York, NY 10010

Copyright © 2014 by The Rosen Publishing Group, Inc.

First Edition

Library of Congress Cataloging-in-Publication Data

Weinick, Suzanne.
Understanding your rights in the information age
/Suzanne Weinick.
      p. cm.—(Personal freedom & civic duty)
Includes bibliographical references and index.
ISBN 978-1-4488-9460-4 (library binding)
1. Civil rights—United States. 2. Internet—Law and legislation—United States. 3. Privacy, Right of—United States. I. Title.
KF4749.W45 2013
342.7308'5—dc23
                                                     2012040221

Manufactured in the United States of America

CPSIA Compliance Information: Batch #S13YA: For further information, contact Rosen Publishing, New York, New York, at 1-800-237-9932.

CONTENTS

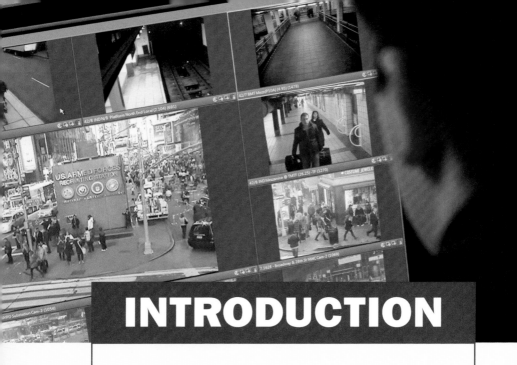

INTRODUCTION

Citizens of the United States of America are fortunate to live in a country that prides itself on protecting individual rights. Yet, with rights come responsibilities. The United States Constitution and the Bill of Rights are the documents that form the basis of the nation's democratic government.

In 1791, the first ten amendments to the Constitution, referred to as the Bill of Rights, became law. The goal of the Bill of Rights is to set limitations on the government's ability to interfere with individual rights and liberties. However, over the years since the Bill of Rights was passed, Americans have challenged many of these personal rights. They have like-wise pressured the federal government to carve

Cyberspace is a new frontier for information and communication. It is also a place where personal information is accessible by not only criminals but also the authorities if there is probable cause.

out exceptions to the freedoms of expression the nation enjoys.

The United States must be careful not to allow fear to lead to the violation of individual constitutional rights. American society encourages debate on issues through free speech, freedom of the press, and dissemination of information. The country frowns upon censorship even if what is said, written, or expressed is hurtful.

When America's Founding Fathers drafted the Constitution, they had no idea about the technological advances that would put a strain on the liberties and privileges citizens value. James Madison, the fourth president of the United States, drafted the Bill of Rights in response to several states requesting more protection for individual liberties in the Constitution. Specifically, the First Amendment contains the language that is the foundation of American democracy. The First Amendment states, "Congress shall make no law respecting an establishment of religion, or prohibiting the free exercise thereof; or abridging the freedom of speech, or of the press; or the right of the people peaceably to assemble, and to petition the government for a redress of grievances." The U.S. Supreme Court is the final authority on how these rights of religion, speech, the press, and assembly will be interpreted so as not to interfere with the other rights protected by the Constitution.

The Fourth Amendment of the U.S. Constitution protects Americans' privacy and prohibits unreasonable searches and seizures of their "persons, houses, papers and effects." Does this prohibition extend to seizure of a person's computer, Facebook postings, or blog entries? The Supreme Court has repeatedly ruled that the right of personal privacy does not extend to public places. However, is a person's Facebook page considered private or public?

The biggest challenge for America is how to preserve its values expressed in the Constitution and Bill of Rights in the face of great technological change. The Internet has made the world a much smaller place by allowing people to communicate more freely and quickly. Yet, it has also changed our perspective on what privacy is and when we can expect in the eyes of the Constitution. The courts, legislators, regulatory agencies, and corporations work together to create a reasonable framework to protect the constitutional rights of Americans while allowing new technology to flourish.

CONSTITUTIONAL FREEDOMS AND PROTECTIONS

The goal of the Bill of Rights, when drafted, was to set limitations on the government's ability to interfere with individual rights. The framers were experienced politicians who knew the importance of providing a flexible constitutional framework that would be interpreted to reflect the needs of a growing and changing country. The concept of separation of powers between the three branches of government, the executive, legislative, and judicial, was to provide the checks and balances necessary to ensure that no one individual or group gained too much power and to protect constitutional liberties.

Specifically, the First Amendment contains the language that is the foundation of our democracy. Freedom of speech, as stated in the First Amendment, is the most basic component of freedom of expression. The U.S. Supreme Court ruled in *Chaplinsky v. New Hampshire* (1942), the so-called "fighting words doctrine," that content of speech can be limited only if such speech would cause a "breach of the peace" or "cause violence."

The U.S. Bill of Rights is a document that protects citizens' individual freedoms and rights. The challenge today is how these principles apply to information in the digital world.

The Internet has ushered in a new era where expression can be in the form of words, pictures, music, and more spread throughout the world in an instant, making it much easier for anyone to incite violence by spreading content over the Web. The First Amendment's protection of freedom of the press is also being challenged in new ways by advances in technology. The press has expanded beyond traditional forms of expression—newspapers, books, television, and radio. The Internet and satellite technology have expanded mass distribution of information.

CLEAR AND PRESENT DANGER

The First Amendment does not protect statements that if uttered would provoke violence or incite illegal action. In *Schenck v. United States* (1919), the Supreme Court ruled that antiwar activists could not hide behind the First Amendment if their words could incite violence during a time of war. The Court said that the character of every act depends on the circumstances in which it is done. This is called the "clear and present danger" test. This test was narrowed in *Abrams v. United States* (1919) to prohibit only speech that creates an imminent threat that requires government intervention.

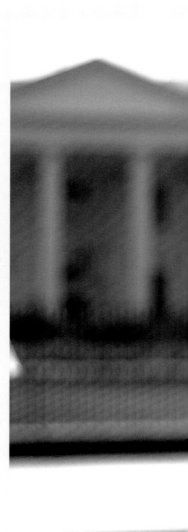

The right to protest government policy and freedom of expression are critical to a democracy and are the essence of America's First Amendment.

The Fourth Amendment of the Bill of Rights also protects individual rights with respect to search and seizure. It prohibits the government from performing unreasonable searches of houses, persons, papers, and effects of individuals. It further provides that if a warrant is sought to authorize a search, there must exist "probable cause." This language is to protect citizens from unnecessary police investigations involving physical searches.

The Fourth Amendment's protections against unreasonable search and seizure have been construed in the context of home searches, stopping and frisking a person in public, and looking through someone's car or private papers, to name a few examples. However, new technologies that can intercept phone and computer transmissions have enabled law enforcement to perform "virtual searches" that do not require physical access to premises, people, or effects. To date, the Supreme Court has not interpreted the Fourth Amendment to apply to the new techniques used to get around traditional searches and seizures.

Limits on the First Amendment

The framers of the U.S. Constitution made clear that "Congress shall make no law . . . abridging the freedom of speech." This has been interpreted to mean that Americans have the freedom to speak publicly and to write and publish their ideas. However, over the years the Supreme Court has limited that freedom in extreme cases to exclude obscenity, hateful speech, and words that cause public panic and dangerous consequences. Yet overall, the U.S. Supreme Court has extended the First Amendment protections of free speech to different forms of expression.

Fighting Words

In *Chaplinsky v. New Hampshire* (1942), the Supreme Court stated that the "English language has a number of words and expressions which by general consent [are] 'fighting words.'" These words include obscenity, profanity, and threats. They are likely to cause a breach of the peace and are therefore not protected by the First Amendment.

Statutes can be written to prohibit this speech as long as they do not interfere with freedom of expression. Most courts have struck down statutes that try to regulate speech based on the "fighting words" ruling of *Chaplinsky* because the language is too broad. On the Internet, "fighting words" are all too common, and since they do not involve face-to-face confrontation, there is little chance that courts will apply this doctrine to online communication.

Note that even if certain language is not prohibited under the protection of the First Amendment, other laws may be violated by the content of the words. For example, a person who threatens to injure another may be charged with harassment. Sending repeated unwanted e-mails to someone can also be construed as harassment.

Obscenity

In *Roth v. United States* (1957), the U.S. Supreme Court ruled that the First Amendment protected art with a sexual theme. The justices decided that the proper test for obscenity is "whether to the average person, applying contemporary community standards, the dominant theme of the material taken as a whole, appeals to the prurient interest." In 1973, another case was decided, *Miller v. California*, in which the Supreme Court determined that states could not outlaw sexually arousing material unless it lacked "serious literary, artistic, political or scientific value." In *Miller*, the Court came up with a three-part test to determine whether expression is "obscene."

The Court again had to make a distinction between speech that was protected for adults but not for children. In *FCC v. Pacifica* (1978), the Supreme Court ruled that the Federal Communications Commission (FCC) could limit broadcasted speech that was "patently offensive" even though such speech in books or theater was not limited. There are numerous cases where the Supreme Court has had to extend the protections of the First Amendment to offensive and hateful speech, actions, and symbols.

Time, Place, and Manner Restrictions

In the past, the courts have had to balance the First Amendment freedom of expression and speech with the need to maintain public safety. These restrictions are content-neutral. A municipality has to be able to set time, place, and manner restrictions on demonstrations, marches, etc., but the government cannot deny access to public spaces, such as streets, parks, and sidewalks. This concept of public forum was noted in *Hague v. CIO* (1939), in which the Supreme Court required that the restrictions of time, place, and manner must be "narrowly tailored to a substantive government interest." This means that an ordinance restricting public meetings must not be arbitrary but rather provide guidelines for permits to assemble in a public place.

The U.S. District Court for the Western District of Oklahoma had to address whether cyberspace is a public forum for First Amendment purposes in *Loving v. Boren* (1997). The court held that cyberspace is not inherently a public forum and therefore the university could not be forced to block access to certain groups. It should be noted, however, that private institutions can prohibit certain speech or expression on their campus.

There is a fine line between creative expression and "hate speech" as defined by many groups advocating

Courts in the United States have had the difficult task of determining how to afford full First Amendment protections to individuals who access computers from public institutions such as universities and libraries.

legislation to limit certain forms of speech. Religious groups have lobbied for protection from speech that rises to the level of defamation of religion. Several Muslim countries have campaigned for the United Nations to adopt a ban on defaming religion. The United States has consistently opposed the ban on defaming religion because it would be a violation of the freedoms of speech, religion, and the press protected by the U.S. Constitution. Civil liberty groups have argued that objective criticism of religion is a protected right of expression. Legislation and litigation are not the best ways to combat hate speech. Strong public opinion and respectful dialogue should be used against such negative expressions.

REDRESS OF GRIEVANCES

The right to petition the government for redress of grievances is the last right granted in the First Amendment of the Constitution. The right to petition for redress of grievances is the right to ask the government to provide relief for a wrong through the courts (by litigation) or other government action. The Founding Fathers wanted to ensure that the public would have the right to communicate their views with federal officials.

This right was important to Thomas Jefferson because he felt this would ensure democracy. The Declaration of Independence was an appeal to the world that the colonists needed to fight British rule after their grievances were ignored by the king and Parliament of England. According to Christopher Phillips, author of *Constitutional Café*, early in our nation's history, U.S. citizens went directly to Congress and literally handed over their petitions and a hearing would be held on their grievances. However, during the Civil War, Congress was flooded with petitions and could no longer hold a hearing on every petition received. This began the dilution of the right to petition the government for redress of grievances. Private citizens rarely gather enough influence through grassroots activities. Professional lobbyists have much more power over the politicians who create our laws.

Groups of Americans who feel wronged by federal policies or laws can petition the government by meeting in public and distributing leaflets on public property. These groups cannot exercise their right to petition for the redress of grievances by trespassing on private property (like a shopping mall or private business establishment). In the case of *NAACP v. Dutton* (1962), the Virginia legislature attempted to prevent the NAACP from providing legal services to individuals whose rights had been violated in school desegregation cases.

However, the Supreme Court concluded that "groups may have no other practical avenue open to petition for redress of grievances" other than through use of the courts. Activist groups face a new threat to their rights of assembly and to petition for redress of grievances in the tools used by the Federal Bureau of Investigation (FBI).

Specifically, the FBI is performing surveillance of computer chats between members of activist groups to check for illegal conduct. However, they are not obtaining search warrants to conduct these electronic searches; they are operating under the authority of the Omnibus Crime Control and Safe Streets Act of 1968, the USA Patriot Act, and the supervision of the U.S. Justice Department. The federal court system is lagging behind in its interpretation of the Fourth Amendment protections of privacy and the use of these advanced surveillance methods.

THE HISTORY OF THE FOURTH AMENDMENT

Privacy from unwanted government intrusion is a fundamental right under the United States Constitution. The colonists were subjected to warrantless searches by British solders, which allowed the soldiers to search any home for any reason. The Fourth Amendment was added to the Bill of Rights to limit the government's ability to enter private property (search) and take property away (seizure). The Founding Fathers were concerned about the collection of private property and privacy of one's house and contents.

The Constitution does not have a clause that specifically guarantees the right to privacy, and the Supreme Court has been vague with its definition of privacy. The Fourth Amendment does completely protect people from searches and seizures. Law enforcement agents are required to obtain a search warrant from a judge or magistrate prior to conducting a search of someone's home unless an exception applies. Search warrants must be supported by "probable cause" that evidence of a crime is present. The search warrant must "particularly describe the place to be searched, and the persons or things to be seized."

In *Olmstead v. United States* (1928), the government secretly monitored the telephone calls of a suspect by "tapping" into the telephone wires. Olmstead claimed that the use of the wiretap was an illegal search and violated his Fourth Amendment right. The Supreme Court decided that the wiretap was not a violation of the defendant's constitutional rights. However, Justice Louis Brandeis disagreed with the majority and said in that case: "The makers of the Constitution undertook to secure conditions favorable to the pursuit of happiness. They conferred, as against the Government, the right to be left alone."

It was not until 1967 that the Supreme Court would read into the words of the Fourth Amendment of the Bill of Rights an expectation of privacy outside one's home. Traditionally, the courts have interpreted the Fourth Amendment protection as applying only to evidence obtained by a government agency when carrying out a physical search. The Supreme Court in *Katz v. United States* made a landmark decision that the Fourth Amendment protects people's expectations of privacy. In this case, the FBI did not obtain a search warrant to listen to someone's conversations in a public phone booth. The Supreme Court ruled that Katz had a reasonable expectation of privacy in the phone booth.

However, the Court has been strict with its interpretation of the Fourth Amendment by viewing the protection in terms of whether there is trespassing or physical intrusion by the government. Police use

technology such as GPS tracking devices to track a person's movements on public thoroughfares and to watch people in public places. This has allowed law enforcement to use video cameras, satellite photography, and tracking devices to conduct investigations on

Prior to the Revolutionary War, colonists were subjected to British "writs of assistance," which were broad search warrants that authorized British custom agents to search and seize private property.

individuals without violating the protections of the Fourth Amendment.

In another case, *Kyllo v. United States* (2001), the Supreme Court determined that the use of a thermal imaging device did constitute a "search" because it was not technology that was "in general public use." The courts seem to draw a distinction when police use binoculars, zoom cameras, and flashlights to look in a house if the general public could do the same from a public street or sidewalk. However, as technology becomes more sophisticated and elaborate, the question becomes, will our expectations of privacy decrease? The Supreme Court is giving law enforcement more power to investigate without fear of having evidence thrown out in court for a violation of the Fourth Amendment.

Even one's personal data and information is not secure from law enforcement investigations if they are stored by a third-party record holder. The Supreme Court decided in *Miller v. United States* (1976) and *Smith v. Maryland* (1979) that an individual takes the risk that information stored by a third-party, such as bank

Thermal imaging is a new technology that can save lives when used by firefighters to locate bodies inside a structure. It can also be used to perform surveillance without a subject's knowledge.

records or telephone statements, are not confidential and can be released to the government without Fourth Amendment search warrant requirements. Therefore, any information a person shares with a private company can be accessed by law enforcement and possibly used against them. Even medical information can be accessed by law enforcement if it shared with a school, employer, or other third party. Most people think that their medical information is not accessible by the federal government. The federal Health Insurance Portability and Accountability Act (HIPAA) sets a national standard for privacy of health information. But HIPAA applies only to medical records maintained by health care providers, health plans, and health care facilities—and only if the facility conducts certain transactions electronically. A great deal of health-related information exists outside of health care facilities and the files of health plans, and thus beyond the reach of HIPAA.

As more and more people conduct business, do their banking, and plan their travel arrangements online, the more data is available to profile individuals without their knowledge and consent. With antiterrorism efforts creating new technologies to prevent and deter attacks, the federal government has authorized new types of intelligence-collecting programs that may reach beyond the scope of the Fourth Amendment's "probable cause" requirements.

In 1968, Congress provided additional protection regarding oral communications under the Fourth Amendment in Title III of the Omnibus Crime Control and Safe Streets Act. This was in response to illegal and abusive surveillance by the FBI. This law requires law enforcement to obtain a Title III wiretap order from a judge to intercept someone's telephone conversations. The rules that apply to wiretaps also apply to bugging a conversation using a hidden electronic device. However, with the introduction of cellular telephone technology, most landline intervention is unnecessary. Cell phone signals can be easily intercepted. In addition, cell phone locations can be tracked. Text messages are also searchable methods of communication because they can easily be intercepted.

The Fourth Amendment concept of privacy is about expectations of the individuals. The Constitution does not contain a specific right to privacy, but the Fourth Amendment relates to the protection of an individual's rights within their private space. The challenge is how to apply the words of the Constitution to new technology.

CONSTITUTIONAL RIGHTS AND CYBERSPACE

Americans have always encouraged people to express their points of view. The Internet has given people a global forum for the free flow of information. With the evolution of the Internet, individuals don't need to write a letter to the editor of a newspaper or call into a radio show to be heard. They can tweet or blog their message to the world.

Freedom of speech gives all individuals the right to post whatever they want even if it is intolerant, hateful, or false. For all these reasons, the digital world is hard to police and monitor. The United States government does not have the authority to censor or control content on the Internet. However, criminal activity must be prosecuted and rights of all individuals should be protected.

The Internet has made it easier for like-minded individuals to communicate. The problem is that the Internet has also been used for harm, such as disseminating hatred by terrorist groups. Web sites created by extremist groups spread hatred and discrimination beyond the scope of traditional press and media. In the

In the past, social networks such as Twitter (www.twitter.com) have challenged court orders to provide information on user identity, citing the users' constitutional protections.

past, a pamphlet handed out on the street may have reached a few thousand people, but hate propaganda on the Internet can reach million. As disturbing as hate speech is, the government does not in general have the right to censor it. The fundamental protection of freedom of speech must include all discussion, even if it is offensive or controversial.

Even though people's rights of freedom of speech are protected by the First Amendment when they express themselves on Facebook and YouTube, that does not mean that they will not feel the consequences if their communications are offensive. Many people have lost their jobs or faced legal action for their expressions. This is true even though the National Labor Relations Board (NLRB), a federal agency, has declared that Facebook posts are legally protected speech.

DEFAMATION

Defamation is disseminating information that is known to be false and intended to harm a person's reputation. Defamation in print is called libel. Defamation in speech is called slander. If a news Web site publishes an article that contains false accusations about a government official or a blogger criticizes public officials, the First Amendment protects them. However, private individuals can sue under defamation laws for knowingly publishing inaccurate statements. Publishing confidential information or trade secrets of a company can also lead to a criminal offense.

In 1996, Congress passed the Communications Decency Act, which provides liability protection to Internet service providers and host sites from being treated as a "publisher" or "speaker" of "any information provided by another information content provider." Web sites that contain information provided by third parties (including blogs, forums, and social networking sites) are protected from defamation claims because they are distributing the information and do not have control of the content. There are limitations to the broad language of the Communications Decency Act liability protections but only for those who edit or publish the information.

INTERNET PORNOGRAPHY

Congress passed the Communications Decency Act (CDA) as part of the Telecommunications Act of 1996, in an attempt to regulate pornographic material on the Internet. A year later, the anti-indecency provision of the CDA was struck down in the Supreme Court case of *Reno v. ACLU* (1997). The Court found that the CDA violated the First Amendment freedom of speech by censoring content online. Congress passed the Child Online Protection Act (COPA) in 1998 to limit potentially harmful content available on the Internet. In 2009, COPA was struck down as unconstitutional by the U.S. Supreme Court because its broad language violated the First Amendment. One area that receives no constitutional protection is child pornography, and law enforcement will use all its resources to catch those that are involved in this type of illegal activity.

ONLINE PRIVACY

The Internet has changed the way people communicate all over the world. Social networking has changed the

Facebook is a great social networking site to connect with friends, but note that nothing online is necessarily deemed by the law as personal and confidential.

way we interact with family, friends, and colleagues. Lori Andrews, an expert on social networks and privacy, says people are drawn to social networks because they provide new ways to interact with a favorite artist, exchange ideas with people who share your interests, and even provide feedback to government agencies. Facebook, Twitter, YouTube, and blogging are the new online places where citizens can voice their opinions and share their thoughts. Social networking sites have become the new place to "hang out" and be heard and seen.

Facebook is currently the most widely used social network in the world with over five hundred million users. It is a place where people can create a network of "friends" to share and communicate with, and keep associations private. Yet, in 2009, Facebook unilaterally changed its privacy policy and made the people listed on one's Facebook page public. Facebook recently settled with the Federal Trade Commission (FTC) for violating users' privacy by changing the privacy settings in a way that made users' personal information more available to the public and Facebook's business partners. In the future, Facebook must get affirmative consent from users prior to changing the privacy settings.

In recent years, public interest groups, such as Electronic Privacy Information Center (EPIC), filed complaints with the FTC and other government agencies on behalf of Internet users for violations of privacy, First Amendment rights, and other civil liberties protected by the Constitution. For example, the FTC has also fined Google over $22 million for violating the default privacy settings by placing advertiser tracking cookies on the Safari browser. In addition, Google is required to submit to independent privacy audits for twenty years from the time of the FTC settlement.

These examples prove that everything people do online is fair game for data miners. Data mining is the process of analyzing information and summarizing it by patterns and relationships. Computers are used to sift through large amounts of data to determine what patterns exist. Grocery chains have been doing this for years to look for shopping patterns in order to forecast trends and predict shopping habits. However, data mining is now a growing industry of searching all the online activities of ordinary people and creating databases with it.

According to the Government Accountability Office (GAO), the Privacy Act of 1974 needs to be revised to reflect technological changes. The GAO has suggested that the federal law is "inadequate to fully protect all personally identifiable information collected, used and maintained by the federal government." Key to the changes recommended by the GAO is that agencies must ensure that the private information collected "is limited to a stated purpose." The GAO recognizes that there is the risk of data breaches at federal agencies and that procedures must be put into place to combat data-mining technologies.

It is important to remember that the First Amendment protections of free speech and the Fourth Amendment's prohibition on unreasonable searches and seizures are restrictions only on actions taken by the government. A private company, on the other hand, can restrict what is said, written, or published by its employees while on the job, and a private amusement park can search all bags coming into its facility. In today's world, Internet companies such as Google and Facebook arguably have more power over the privacy and free speech of most users than the U.S. government. Jeffrey Rosen, author and editor of *Constitution 3.0, Freedom and Technological Change*, says the true challenge confronting millions of people around the world is "how best to live our lives in a world where the Internet records everything and forgets nothing, where every online photo, status update, Twitter post, and blog entry by and about us can be stored forever."

EXPECTATIONS OF PRIVACY

The Fourth Amendment refers to "papers and effects" as the items that a person would have securely in their homes in colonial times. Today, one's personal records and information are on cell phones, in computers, and stored by doctors and financial institutions. The computer is among the greatest technological advances in history, and yet, it is also among the greatest threats to personal privacy.

Cell phones transmit voice through satellites and therefore are not as secure as a traditional landline telephone. Therefore, people have little expectation of privacy when it comes to cell phone conversations.

Data transmitted through cell phones and smartphones is not necessarily secure from interception by both criminals and other parties that seek to gather information.

This is one example of how people have adjusted their expectations when it comes to the conveniences of new technology. In a research study cited by Christopher Slobogin in *Constitution 3.0*, more people indicated that it was more intrusive for the government to access someone's bank account, credit card, and telephone records than physically to search someone's car. However, under the current case law, the search of a car requires "probable cause" under the Fourth Amendment but access to personal records does not. This suggests that the courts, legislature, and government agencies are lagging behind the new ways in which law enforcement conducts surveillance. The potential risk to constitutional freedom in the information age is that the government

BORDER CAMERAS

In November 2008, the state of Texas installed security cameras to alert authorities of any illegal immigrants crossing the border. Anyone with an Internet connection could watch the cameras by logging on to the Web site and report any suspicious activity to the sheriff's office. The site had over 130,000 "Virtual Texas Deputies" watching for illegal immigrants in its first year, sending thousands of e-mails to the sheriff's office each week. However, the border camera project resulted in only twenty-six arrests after two years.

Civil liberties groups worry that this type of surveillance will lead to vigilantism. The social network BlueServo, which powered the Web site in Texas, has other public cameras around the country that stream live feeds on the Internet. This type of neighborhood watch surveillance potentially leads to an invasion of privacy by capturing people doing routine activities in their neighborhoods. It can also lead to citizens taking law enforcement into their own hands if they view illegal activity.

Since the September 11, 2001, terrorist attacks, the number of video surveillance cameras around the country has skyrocketed. They are used to enhance public safety but can also infringe on the public's rights of privacy.

could gain too much power to access information about ordinary citizens without proving it has a reason to collect such data.

During the so-called Great Recession, many municipalities around the country installed public surveillance cameras to deter criminal activity and obtain evidence of traffic violations. City officials justify the use of these cameras as a cost saving measure because fewer police officers are needed to patrol when cameras provide additional information. Surveillance of citizens conducting their daily activity in public places is becoming commonplace, but is it an invasion of privacy? Surveillance cameras are legal because a person on a public street has no expectation of privacy. According to Mark Schlosberg of the American Civil Liberties Union (ACLU) of Northern California, "The average person is photographed over 300 times a day" in London, England, where cameras were installed around the city. These statistics were cited in a 2012 report of the American Civil Liberties Union of Michigan. The ACLU questions the cost-effectiveness and efficiency of crime fighting by using video surveillance cameras all around a city. The city of Lansing, Michigan, instituted the use of video cameras in 2008, but very few crimes were prevented or solved with the use of the surveillance cameras. The ACLU warns that the

DIGITAL TRACKING

Radio frequency identification devices (RFID) are a type of identification tracking technology. Small computer chips are inserted in packages, books, ID cards, and merchandise. The RFID must be scanned to get the identifying information but it does not require contact with the person carrying the item.

Many companies use RFIDs to keep tabs on inventory or employees entering and leaving the office. The concern is when this technology is used secretly without an employee or consumer knowing that they are being tracked with these devices. Collectively, these devices will put us under constant surveillance and will erode our privacy.

private information captured by the cameras is a violation of privacy of innocent people and an ineffective use of police resources.

Employees are watched via cameras in their work environment; patrons are monitored in hotels, office buildings, and restaurants; and satellites provide visual images of people in parks, at concerts, and even at religious or political events. Americans are being watched more than they realize, and under the current interpretation of the Fourth Amendment, these virtual searches are not prohibited or regulated.

THE FREEDOM OF INFORMATION ACT

In 1966, Congress enacted the Freedom of Information Act (FOIA), which allows any person the right, enforceable in court, to obtain access to federal agency records. The exception is if such records (or portions of them) are protected from public disclosure by one of nine exemptions or by one of three special law enforcement record exclusions. Even non-U.S. citizens can request documents from a federal agency. In 1996, the federal FOIA was amended to extend to electronic records of government agencies. In addition, all states have freedom of information or open record laws to make information available to the public.

In 2009, President Barack Obama issued a memorandum to the heads of executive departments and agencies emphasizing "accountability through transparency" in enforcing the FOIA. Specifically, President Obama said in his memorandum that the presumption of disclosure also means that "agencies should take affirmative steps to make information public." Yet, there is no centralized place to access federal government information. A FOIA request must be made to the specific agency that has the documents being searched for. Federal agencies have twenty days to respond to FOIA requests and must provide the specific statutory exemption that applies if your request is denied.

However, there are limitations on Freedom of Information Act requests. Most important and controversial are exemptions deemed "classified" for national security.

In recent years, the exemptions to public access to information have increased because of privacy concerns. Many of these exemptions protect individuals from disclosure of personal information. Bank and financial institution records are exempt, as are medical records maintained by insurance companies and health care providers. Students' educational records are also protected by federal privacy laws.

INDIVIDUAL RIGHTS AND DIGITAL MEDIA

Media choices have grown tremendously over the last thirty years, and the Internet has created places where any political, social, or religious group can find an audience for its ideas. Media outlets—television, radio, magazines, newspapers, and the Internet— are competing for people's attention every minute of every day. Search engines sort Web sites by storing and retrieving content. News anchors, network commentators, and talk-show hosts are constantly expressing strong viewpoints that are designed to spark debate. The audience, viewers, and listeners of all these differing opinions must determine what information is credible and thoughtful.

PRIVACY VS. THE PRESS

Media is everywhere in the information age. With the twenty-four-hour news cycle, there is much more competition to get the "hot" sensational story. An issue of privacy arises when private individuals get thrown into the spotlight and unwillingly become "news." In *The Right to Privacy*, authors Ellen Alderman and Caroline

With the aggressiveness of the twenty-four-hour cable news cycle, the rights of freedom of the press and individuals' right to privacy have often been at odds.

Kennedy point out the conflict between a person's right to privacy in his or her private life and the American ideal of an "open and outspoken press." The press oversteps its bounds when it invades people's privacy in the name of digging up gossip or a sensational story. The Founding Fathers considered a free press to be a watchdog of government and not designed to trample on individuals' rights of privacy.

However, the Supreme Court has historically protected the First Amendment protection of uninhibited and wide-open debate of public issues. The *New York*

Times ran an advertisement that criticized the way nonviolent protesters were treated by police in Montgomery, Alabama. The advertisement included statements, some of which were false, about police action allegedly directed against students who participated in a civil rights demonstration and against a leader of the civil rights movement. The respondent, L. B. Sullivan, commissioner of public affairs of Montgomery, Alabama, claimed the statements referred to him because his duties included supervision of the police department.

L. B. Sullivan, sued the *New York Times* for libel to protect his reputation. In *The New York Times v. Sullivan* (1964), the court held that no public official may recover damages for a defamatory falsehood relating to his official conduct unless he proves that the statement was made with "actual malice." The Court defined actual malice as "with knowledge that it was false or with reckless disregard of whether it was false or not." This means that you have more latitude to criticize government officials than you would for speaking falsely about a private individual.

Famous people also must prove "actual malice" to recover for libel. In *Gertz v. Robert Welch, Inc.* (1974), the Supreme Court decided that people who have fame or notoriety must meet the same standard as public figures to prove false statements were knowingly made against them. The standard of proving "actual malice" is only when dealing with a public official or public figure. *The New York Times v. Sullivan* does not apply when the media discussion involves a private individual. In *Gertz v. Robert Welch, Inc.*, the Court held that states can hold publishers or broadcasters to a lower standard of liability for defamatory falsehood that causes actual injury to a private individual.

INVASION OF PRIVACY

The Fourth Amendment right of privacy is a protection of individual citizens from abuses by the government. When an individual or member of the press violates the privacy of a private individual, the legal cause of action is invasion of privacy, which is a civil tort, an intentional or negligent wrongful act causing personal injury or harm.

The common law tort of invasion of privacy is broken down into four torts—intrusion, private facts, false light, and appropriation—as defined by legal scholar William Prosser in 1960. Again, the Supreme Court has had difficulty in applying the principles of these torts to invasion of privacy cases. However, the test is to prove the information has been used in a manner that is "highly offensive to a reasonable person." Even if the Court finds that the press or an individual violated someone's right to privacy in tort law, what is the legal remedy for hurt feelings and embarrassment?

The toughest challenges are when the right to privacy in tort law comes up against the freedom of the press protected by the First Amendment. The public wants to know everything about an incriminating e-mail written by a public figure, but the average person doesn't want his or her own private information distributed in public. This is the classic conflict between privacy and the press.

COPYRIGHT LAWS

Anyone who creates an original work (e.g., a book, movie, piece of music, or work of art) has the legal right to protect that work under copyright laws. Once the work has been created and published, anyone using, copying, or distributing that property without permission

Google and other search engines house user information, which has raised the question about who owns the copyright to users' data that is stored on their servers.

may be infringing on the creator's rights. When the term of the copyright expires, the work goes into the public domain and may be freely used. Again, the single largest challenge to preventing piracy of copyrighted material is the Internet and new technology that makes it difficult to prevent violations of the copyright laws.

In 1998, Congress passed the Digital Millennium Copyright Act (DMCA), which comprehensively changed U.S. copyright law. The use of search engine portals, blogs, social networking sites, and video-sharing sites (such as YouTube) have created a need to protect intellectual property to keep up with the new technology. The DMCA was designed to prevent consumers from going around copyright protections and to provide immunity to companies hosting the content. The way that the law works is if someone posts a movie clip on YouTube, YouTube is the company hosting the content and would not be liable for copyright infringement if it removes the material once the copyright holder sends a takedown notice that such posting is an infringement.

The entertainment industry has filed many lawsuits against YouTube, Google, and Facebook for copyrighted material being used without permission, but the courts have not been consistent in deciding what is "fair use" under the DMCA.

The Internet is a wide-open forum for exchanging ideas and information. Even though much of the information found on the Internet is available for public use, it may still have copyright protection. Therefore, before one copies or scans material from another source, it is worth getting permission from the author or owner to ensure that you do not violate copyright laws.

INTERNET SPEECH

Communication transmitted over the Internet is protected speech under the Constitution. In *Reno v. ACLU* (1997), the Supreme Court applied the First Amendment protections to speech on the Internet. The Court has also held that the right of free speech and a free press means that the speaker can choose what to say and what not to say.

Search engines such as Google and Yahoo! sort and filter search results for its users. Articles and opinions in newspapers and periodicals are edited and printed at the discretion of the publisher. Search results on Internet search engines are organized based on algorithms that are created to reflect the content and information available for that word or phrase on the Internet. However, the algorithms can be manipulated to cause inappropriate results to top the search list. There has been criticism that search engine companies should be held accountable when the Internet

is used to tamper with search results.

While search engine companies compare themselves to newspapers and periodicals, others believe that the manipulation of search results by search engine companies results in unfair competition by favoring their own site over those of competitors. The search engine companies have the ability to filter results that are offensive, but the question is whether using the filtering tool is a form of censorship of the Internet.

However, search engine companies are providing a service and should not be treated like individuals exercising their rights of free speech. Like newspaper editors, search engines have the right to organize and prioritize material while still being protected by the First

In protest of several bills proposed in Congress that potentially threatened free speech, a number of Internet companies, such as Wikipedia (www.wikipedia.org), staged an online "blackout," a temporary shutdown of services, on January 18, 2012.

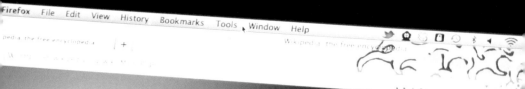

Imagine a World Without Free Knowledge

For over a decade, we have spent millions of hours building the largest encyclopedia in human history. Right now, the U.S. Congress is considering legislation that could fatally damage the free and open Internet. For 24 hours, to raise awareness, we are blacking out Wikipedia. Learn more.

Contact your representatives.

Your ZIP code:

MacBook Pro

Amendment—freedom of the press. Two federal courts have issued opinions that have determined that Google has full constitutional protection even though it decides what content, advertising, and results are displayed when a user conducts a search.

Two bills are being considered in Congress to stop illegal copying and sharing of movies, music, and other copyrighted material. Many Internet companies object to the legislation because it would make them responsible for content that is out of their control. The user-generated encyclopedia Wikipedia, Google, Facebook, Twitter, and hundreds of other Internet sites organized an Internet blackout in protest on January 18, 2012. The purpose of the blackout was to educate Internet users about the threats to online speech and the open exchange of ideas on the Web. It was to protest pending congressional legislation to prevent copyright infringement on the Internet.

THE PRICE OF FAME

Even if you are not a rock star, movie star, or public figure, you have probably been photographed and videotaped more than you realize. Every day, citizens capture crime scenes, embarrassing situations, and natural disasters with their camera phones. Many of these images and videos end up on Web sites, including YouTube, Facebook, and Twitter. Is there any expectation of privacy when you are in public?

WIKILEAKS

WikiLeaks is one of many Web sites that publish classified or sensitive government documents on the Internet. Julian Assange, publisher of WikiLeaks, allowed U.S. State Department messages about foreign policy to be published on his Web site. Is this type of information dissemination protected by the freedom of the press clause of the First Amendment?

According to many, the answer is yes, WikiLeaks should be afforded the same rights as traditional news-gathering agencies and outlets. The framers of the Constitution did not define the "press" to a specific medium, and therefore, Congress cannot limit the press freedom clause. The real issue with WikiLeaks is that it has published classified information. Many feel that releasing these government documents has endangered our national security and may have put American troops at risk during the war in Afghanistan. The Justice Department is considering whether to prosecute WikiLeaks and Assange under the Espionage Act.

Most states have laws prohibiting certain types of public privacy violations. For example, it would be an offense to photograph someone in a changing room or bathroom. There is a universal expectation of privacy in these settings because there is no competing interest at stake. In these cases, it is not hard to prove that the intrusion was "highly offensive to a reasonable person." However, when your friends post photographs of you on the Internet from a party or concert, you have little control over those images.

Many celebrities complain that aerial images of their homes is a violation of their privacy, but the Superior Court of California has held that "aerial views are a common part of daily life." Google maps using satellite technology makes aerial photographs available on its Web site.

CYBERBULLYING

In our digital world, bullying occurs online even more frequently than in person. Many states have passed antibullying legislation, but legal experts worry that some of these laws have gone too far and are impeding freedom of speech. The law must be specific so that the offender knows what behavior will not be tolerated. Most school antibullying policies consider any communication that is unwanted, demeaning, or belittling to be subject to discipline. Any negative online communication between students that results in a disruption in someone's ability to do their schoolwork could result in disciplinary action.

All texts, photos, and video captured on cell phones or downloaded to computers can become electronic evidence against you if you commit a crime or civil offense using your electronic devices.

In order to protect your computer and cell phone from being used against you by unauthorized users, make sure you create a password or pin that unlocks the keyboard. Don't give your e-mail or cell phone number to anyone you don't know and report any suspicious conversations to adults and, if necessary, to the police.

POLITICAL CORRECTNESS

The United States has been grappling for over two centuries with creating a country based on equality. When discussing race, gender, politics, sexual orientation, or religion, our nation has been outspoken on what words are considered politically correct to use in context of these areas.

Beginning in the 1960s, the movement for equal rights for American Indians experienced a linguistic change and became a movement for equal rights for "Native Americans." However, by the 1990s, there was a backlash that political correctness was causing Americans to become emotionally upset about any comments made in the media that were perceived by a group as victimizing them. The effect was threatening the rights protecting free speech. In 1991, President George H. W. Bush called politically correct thinking "bullying" by declaring "certain topics off-limits, certain expressions off-limits, even certain gestures off-limits." The president went on to say that the politically correct movement had gone too far. He concluded: "What began as a crusade for

Journalist Juan Williams was fired from his job at National Public Radio (NPR) for statements he made about Muslims and terrorism on a Fox News program in 2010.

civility has soured into a cause of conflict and even censorship."

Juan Williams, a journalist who was fired by National Public Radio (NPR) for comments he made about Muslims, claims that the growth of media outlets has created a more fractionalized country. While the country has grown diverse, there is little compromise in the conversation between groups. Williams says: "Hypersensitivity and supercharged responses to the slightest of perceived transgressions are now the norm." This has resulted in each group claiming to be victim to violations of political correctness and is another attempt to stifle free speech.

However, according to Juan Williams, the media personalities are not "on the air to compromise or bring opposing sides together." They are offering provocative commentary to get higher ratings and please their target audience. Williams says that the current state of media is actually "stifling the genuine give-and-take of honest debate." Criticism of the way the media is constantly perpetuating conflict between political extremes centers around the way these commentators are playing to hate, fear, and personal attacks on opposing points of view.

America's Founding Fathers wanted the freedoms of the First Amendment to promote education, democracy, and a tolerant society. When these freedoms are used to inhibit the function of government and

FactCheck.org | A Project of the Annenberg Public Policy

Check.org | A Project of the...   +

www.factcheck.org

FACTCHECK.ORG

A PROJECT OF THE ANNENBERG PUBLIC POLICY CENTER

Home   Featured   The Wire   Ask FactCheck   Mailbag   Viral Spiral   Archives   About Us

Obama's Numbers

Statistical measures of the president's term to date.

THE WIRE

Group's 'Obamacare Tax Form' Evades Facts

November 16

A conservative group misleads taxpayers on the Affordable Care Act and the Internal Revenue Service's future role in enforcing it. Americans for Tax Reform posted a "projected" IRS tax form on its website that claims to "help families and tax specialists prepare" for new tax provisions under the health care ...
More >>

Facts Falling Off the Fiscal Cliff

November 14

In press conferences on the so-called fiscal cliff, House Speaker John Boehner greatly exaggerated the negative effect on the economy of raising taxes on upper-income individuals. Boehner erred

FEATURED ARTICLES

* 3. I found the information on the site t

○ Strongly Agree

○ Agree

○ Disagree

○ Strongly Disagree

Our Subscribers Speak

Most say we're clear, accurate, useful and un
November 14
Summary Once again, FactCheck.org's subscribers find our articles to be clear, unbiased, accurate and results of our latest post-election survey are similar t from surveys we conducted after the presidential ele 2004 and 2008. In all three surveys, 99 percent said
...
More >>

FactCheck.org (www.factcheck.org) is a nonprofit consumer watchdog Web site that aims to assist citizens in understanding the facts behind politicians' claims.

November

NUMBERS

In the interest of timeliness and accuracy, we are issuing an updated version of "Obama's Numbers," our collection of key measures of the president's time in office. A few things have changed since we published our original version Oct. 8 — some for better, and some for worse. The number ...

The 2012 FactCheck Awards

Our Election-Day sampler of funny, scary an bizarre campaign ads.

Dictionary defines "political correctness" to mean "the

FACTCHECK

Is Lockheed Martin going to lay off
000 workers because of President
ma's downsizing of the military?

No. Lockheed gave a "very rough"
nate of 10,000 potential layoffs (not
000) due to automatic spending cuts
ered by a 2011 bipartisan deficit-
ction bill. Obama and Congress are
tiating to avoid the cuts.

Read the full question and answer
View the Ask FactCheck archives

DONATE

Help us
hold politicians
accountable.

your knowledge.
our weekly game.

View the Quiz archives

_ **SPIRAL**

't get spun by Internet rumors.

View the FactCheck FAQ

CHECK MAILBAG

heck Mailbag, Week of Oct. 30-Nov. 5

**FactCheck has been an
invaluable tool to me this**

prevent honest and open debate on policies affecting our nation, then these rights are being abused. The First Amendment gives everyone in the United States the right to speak freely without government censorship or reprisal. Underlying this right is that the speech will be honest and truthful.

WHO'S CHECKING THE FACTS?

FactCheck.org is an independent political watchdog group that checks the facts politicians use in their political statements, in ads, in press releases, and on their Web sites. Holding politicians accountable for telling the truth and being honest has always been important to the American public. As a nonprofit, nonpartisan organization, the mission of

FactCheck.org is to be a consumer advocate for voters. It monitors the factual accuracy of local, state, and federal politicians.

Advances in technology have made it very difficult for the average person to determine what news sources are credible and unbiased. Gone are the days when only a few network television stations provided the bulk of the news coverage. Cable television has numerous stations that provide twenty-four-hour news. Added to this are satellite radio, Web sites, and blogs providing more information. Newspapers cannot compete with the speed of news delivered via the Internet. The problem is that many Americans do not know the credibility of the sources they use to get the news they need to make an informed decision on important issues.

TECHNOLOGY AND PRIVACY

Technology is changing the way we communicate, exchange information, and purchase daily products. Many of these new technologies have made positive impacts on our productivity in the workplace and in personal interactions with friends and family. However, some of these modern conveniences are jeopardizing personal privacy. According to David H. Holtzman, author of *Privacy Lost: How Technology Is Endangering Your Privacy*, every human transaction is being stored. Since privacy is about information control, the public should be concerned that computerized technology has caused people to lose control of private information. Holtzman warns that "the balance between national security and privacy has tipped precariously toward security."

BIG BROTHER IS WATCHING YOU

George Orwell warned in his book *1984* to beware of a government that is watching its citizens' every move. The federal government is working on various systems to track citizens and

In this scene from a movie adaptation of George Orwell's novel *1984*, Big Brother, symbolizing an authoritarian government, is always watching the citizens.

review data to uncover terrorist activities. Yet, the biggest threat to individual privacy comes from private companies using their databases to collect and distribute private information. We are constantly hearing on the news about massive data breaches caused by employees of banks, credit card companies, and online services mishandling customers' information. The legislature and the courts have not determined how to hold these institutions and private companies responsible for protecting privacy. According to David Holtzman, "The law will always lag behind technology."

Law enforcement can access a person's electronic communications by obtaining a subpoena for the information. The government has to demonstrate only that the information likely to be obtained is relevant to an ongoing criminal investigation. The subpoena will give them basic subscriber information, but to get your e-mail log of whom you sent and received messages to and from, the law enforcement agency needs to secure a "D Order" (a subsection of the Stored Communications Act). The subscriber is supposed to be given prior notice before a D Order or subpoena is used to obtain the content of e-mails. Notice is not required if law enforcement gets a search order from a judge to get the information.

The Internet and Personal Information

The Internet is public and therefore accessible to anyone who goes online. It is not just the government that is interested in what citizens are doing online; businesses are tracking customers every time they click the mouse on the computer. There are numerous companies that are creating huge databases that

Certain products from Internet companies, such as Chromebook, a computer operating system from Google, are designed to collect as much information as possible from their users.

cross-reference the information people search for on the Internet. When you visit a Web site, you leave a trail of your preferences. Analyzing online activity of consumers is an important marketing tool in the information age.

You think you have total privacy when you are surfing the Web on your home computer. However, virtually all Web sites have tracking software, and many sites record your activity within the site. The Internet service provider (ISP) that you subscribe to in order to connect to the Internet tracks your online activity. Web browsers (such as Firefox or Google Chrome) also store your activity on Web sites. The information collected about you is used to create an individual profile about the way you conduct searches and make purchases. Your ISP and Web browser will provide advertisers and retailers with your profile information to target products and services that would interest you. None of this sounds devious, but you should be aware that your IP (Internet protocol) address and search preferences are not private and may be used by third parties without your knowledge.

What about hackers who gain access to computer systems through the Internet to steal information or cause problems with your computer? These Internet predators are smart, creative people who are looking to steal your personal and financial information. They can send e-mails requesting your bank account

IDENTITY THEFT

Identity theft is when someone illegally acquires and uses another person's personal information. The thief steals your Social Security number, credit card number, and/or name and address to withdraw funds from your bank account, purchase items using your credit card, or secure a loan in your name. Victims of identity theft spend years clearing their financial reputation and credit history.

Identity theft is the fastest growing crime in the United States and is the leading cause of consumer fraud. Millions file identity theft complaints with the Federal Trade Commission (FTC) every year.

To protect yourself from becoming a victim of identity theft, you should not share your Social Security number, bank account information, or personal information with anyone other than an employer or a known and trusted business that you contact directly. In addition, you should shred your junk mail and make sure you use a secure connection when using the Internet.

information, create computer programs that access files on your computer, and tap into your Wi-Fi connection while you are at Starbucks. You can protect your privacy by setting up a firewall on your computer to block unauthorized access and installing antivirus software. It is also a good idea to create passwords for accessing Web sites that contain your important information.

Malware and Internet Viruses

An innocent search on an Internet search engine can lead you to jeopardize your computer and your privacy. It was recently reported that Emma Watson, actress in the Harry Potter movies, is the favorite celebrity bait for cyber criminals trying to lure Internet users. According to an Associated Press article, when searching for Emma Watson on the Internet, "there's a one-in-eight chance of landing on a malicious site." This is why it is important to safeguard your computer equipment with software that scans for cyber attacks.

Collection of Information

New technology in surveillance and data collection is creating an issue of intrusion into personal information. If a government agency has access to

Internet companies often store their users' data on massive servers, such as these at Google, for periods of time and sometimes indefinitely despite criticism from privacy advocates.

private information and discloses it to a third party (public or private), there is the opportunity for the information to be abused or misused. For example, the Internal Revenue Service (IRS) collects information through the tax filing database. Individuals have to include their addresses, Social Security numbers, and other private information. An employee of the IRS or other federal government agency can obtain this information through computer access and distribute it to persons looking to create fraudulent credit card accounts. The U.S. government must protect the information it collects from intentional or unintentional distribution and abuse.

Personal information about our shopping habits and preferences are collected when we purchase items at the grocery or retail store. Point-of-sale scanning creates a data profile about when you shop, what you buy, and what price you pay. This information is passed on to manufacturers, advertisers, and marketing firms. Even the electronic devices that collect tolls from drivers via a prepaid account are recording where your vehicle has been and the exact time that you traveled.

Most people don't feel violated by the collection of their personal information if it will make their lives easier. However, when the information collected is distributed to third parties, it may be a violation of your privacy rights. The global network of databases that

BIOMETRICS

Biometrics is the science of using human traits and characteristics to identify a person. New technological advances have created systems that recognize people based on characteristics such as fingerprints or the eye's iris, or behavioral traits, such as voice patterns. Biometrics can be used to enhance security and prevent fraud related to personal identity. Even Disney World in Orlando, Florida, is using fingerprint recognition when it admits patrons to its amusement parks.

The Federal Bureau of Investigation (FBI) is working on its Next Generation Identification (NGI) Facial Recognition Program. This program will initially contain a database of at least twelve million photos that can be identified as specific individuals. The FBI is planning on using this database to search and identify people in crowds even if those people have not committed a crime or are suspected of a crime. Additionally, the FBI is in negotiations with other countries to share information. This type of biometric data collection and distribution creates serious concerns of individual privacy.

have access to personal records is a growing problem around the world. Federal and state governments do not fully understand the technology involved and, therefore, have not created a set of laws that properly protect the average citizen from intrusion into their personal information. In many instances, in order to keep your address, telephone number, or e-mail

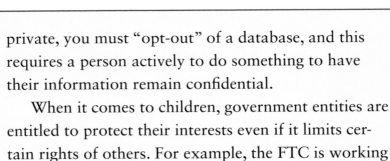

private, you must "opt-out" of a database, and this requires a person actively to do something to have their information remain confidential.

When it comes to children, government entities are entitled to protect their interests even if it limits certain rights of others. For example, the FTC is working on the Children's Online Privacy Protection Rule, which gives parents control over what information Web sites and online services may collect from children under thirteen.

FINGERPRINTS TO DNA TESTING

Since the early nineteenth century, law enforcement has used fingerprinting to identify criminals. In 1953, the discovery of DNA led to the identification of the thousands of genes in human DNA. The information available has many positive benefits. New tests can indicate whether you have inherited a medical disorder or a predisposition to get a disease. Such information can also be used by employers or insurance companies, and this could have a negative impact on a person's life. Genetic test results should be private information. A majority of state legislatures have enacted genetic antidiscrimination laws. Most of these states prohibit health and life insurance companies from using genetic information to determine someone's risk of becoming ill.

Biometric scanners use unique physical or behavioral traits to identify a person. Examples of this technology are security systems that use fingerprint, handwriting, or face recognition scanners.

DNA testing has been useful for the criminal justice system. Many criminals have been prosecuted based on DNA evidence connecting them to a crime scene or a crime victim. In addition, DNA evidence has been used to secure the release of innocent convicted prisoners. Betsy Kuhn points out in her book *Prying Eyes: Privacy in the Twenty-First Century* that the most recent trend is taking DNA samples from arrestees who have not been convicted of a crime. The question is whether this practice is constitutional since arrestees are innocent until proven guilty. Civil liberties advocates believe DNA tests should not be done just to increase DNA databases.

SOCIAL NETWORKING AND SOCIAL MEDIA

Social media includes Web- and mobile-based technologies used to create interactive communities. Individuals connect with friends, colleagues, and like-minded groups to

Social networking sites are branching out into business. Sites such as LinkedIn (www.linkedin.com) may help you find a job, but they also collect users' information just like any other social network.

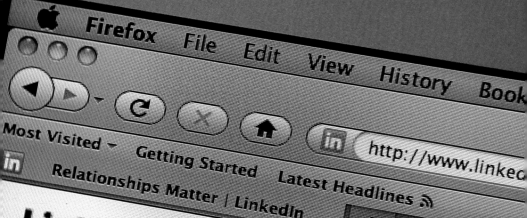

share information, opinions, and photographs on social networking sites (like Facebook, LinkedIn, and YouTube).

Since social media is a two-way communication tool, it is becoming an integral part our daily lives. Sharing on social networking sites should be done with minimum expectation of privacy. Do not post pictures that you would not want to see on the cover of your local paper. Refrain from speaking negatively about your friends, teachers, and work colleagues. Do not put your address and telephone number in your contact information online. Even if you restrict your Facebook profile to "friends only," you should assume that everyone has access to your information. Use discretion when putting pictures or other content on your social networking sites. People have been denied jobs or admission to college because of the pictures and words they have on their profile page.

Social media has also become a news-gathering tool for journalists, according to Ashley Messenger, associate general counsel for National Public Radio. However, Messenger warns that the information posts, tweets, and photographs may be protected by copyright laws, and journalists would need to get permission from the person who first published the information. Social media groups (e.g., blogs and chat rooms) must be protected as cybergatherings just like meetings in a public square two hundred years ago. The speech conducted in these Web-based forums need the same protection under the First Amendment rights of assembly and free speech.

The right to privacy does not have to be diminished in order for us to enjoy modern technology. All Americans must be informed consumers and read the agreements they are asked to sign by companies that retain their personal information. With increased media attention on privacy concerns on the Internet and social media sites, more Americans are evaluating their privacy settings on such sites. According to a Pew Research Center survey, "54 percent of mobile users have decided not to install an app after discovering the amount of information it collects." This proves that more consumers are paying attention to violations of their privacy.

Mobile devices and mobile Internet connections create additional privacy concerns. Using the Internet through a wireless connection exposes your personal information to interception.

NATIONAL SECURITY AND CIVIL LIBERTIES

The terrorist attacks on the United States on September 11, 2001, were a wake-up call to all Americans that global terrorism could strike at any time. Since 9/11, when the United States suffered from terrorist attacks on American soil, the federal government's response has been to increase surveillance powers at the expense of civil liberties. The USA Patriot Act implemented measures that were supposed to provide tools to combat terrorism and threats to our national security. In addition, several months after the 9/11 attacks, President George W. Bush signed an executive order allowing the National Security Agency (NSA) to eavesdrop on international telephone calls and to monitor international e-mails of people in the United States. Spying by American intelligence agencies is not a new phenomenon, but the lack of judicial oversight of these operations is increasing. Collecting personal information on people and eavesdropping on conversations is overreaching government power and violates the Constitution.

THE PATRIOT ACT AND NATIONAL SECURITY

Many United States citizens have been living in fear of terrorism since the attacks on 9/11. President Bush responded to this concern by pushing through Congress the USA Patriot Act, enabling law enforcement agencies to perform what some would argue to be aggressive surveillance and crackdowns on protesters in the name of public safety. The USA Patriot Act contains a broad definition of "domestic terrorism"

The First Amendment protects the right of the people to peaceably assemble. Civil protests are a type of freedom of expression.

and increases the wiretapping powers for government agencies. This allows the FBI to read people's e-mails and listen to telephone conversations.

In addition, the USA Patriot Act also expands the National Security Letter (NSL) power, giving the FBI and other agencies the ability to bypass courts and obtain almost any personal information from banks, Internet service providers, and credit card companies. The NSL statutes allow the FBI to issue administrative letters demanding information about a customer.

The NSL statutes further implement a "gag order" on the service provider from informing the customer that the request for records has been made. This makes it hard to litigate objections to the demand for information because the customer does not even know about it. However, using the Freedom of Information Act, the Electronic Frontier Foundation (EFF) and American Civil Liberties Union (ACLU) have exposed abuses of the NSL power by the FBI. If the courts allow the USA Patriot Act and the NSL

The American Civil Liberties Union (ACLU) is a not-for-profit organization that protects individual rights and liberties through litigation, legislation, and advocacy.

statutes to stand, privacy over our effects will be severely compromised.

The USA Patriot Act extended government electronic surveillance without judicial review. It is an open-ended limitation on the protections of the Bill of Rights. For example, government agents can listen in on conversations between lawyers and their clients in federal prisons without a prior court order. This is a clear violation of the attorney/client privilege, which our courts have consistently held to be a private communication. This type of spying on American citizens and watering down of our constitutional protections will not bring an end to international terrorism or domestic threats of violence.

Author and reporter Nat Hentoff is extremely concerned about overreaching government power, especially by the U.S. Department of Justice, after 9/11. In particular, Hentoff focused on Operation TIPS—the Terrorism Information and Prevention System, which would have recruited letter carriers, meter readers, cable technicians, and other workers with access to private homes to report any suspicious activity to the Justice Department. However, the Homeland Security bill, which became law in 2002, prohibited federal programs that would promote the spying of citizens on one another and Operation TIPS was officially eliminated.

In our technologically advanced society, activists organize their activities online and by mobile phone. This makes it easier for law enforcement to spy on this type of activity. According to the Center for Constitutional Rights (CCR), government protesters run the risk of being "arrested and prosecuted for their First Amendment activities under so-called material support laws." The material support statutes are part of the USA Patriot Act and makes it a crime to provide support—including humanitarian aid, literature distribution, and peaceful political advocacy—to any entity that the government has designated as a "terrorist" group.

The USA Patriot Act "material support" statutes were tested in the 2010 Supreme Court case *Holder v. Humanitarian Law Project.* In this case, the Court ruled that providing training and assistance to groups on the government's list of terrorist groups can be prosecuted under the Patriot Act. The decision reached in this case puts limits on the constitutional right to protest and dissent our government's policies. The First Amendment protects freedom of speech and press, the right of people to peaceably assemble, and the right to petition the government for a redress of grievances.

The prohibition against government eavesdropping on American citizens has been documented throughout our country's history. Anthony D.

Romero's book *In Defense of Our America* points out the federal government has been collecting information on the ACLU's activities since 9/11. Also targeted were environmental groups such as Greenpeace and antiwar groups such as United for Peace and Justice. Even student activists were on the Defense Department's TALON (the Threat and Local Observance Notice) list.

The Internet can be a dangerous place due to cyber-criminals. Software companies and Internet service providers are always working on new ways to protect consumers' computers from these threats.

CYBERSECURITY

The federal government is working on creating a cybersecurity act that would provide government-mandated security standards for key infrastructure businesses (such as power companies) to prevent hackers from attacking their computer networks. It will also establish a protocol to share critical

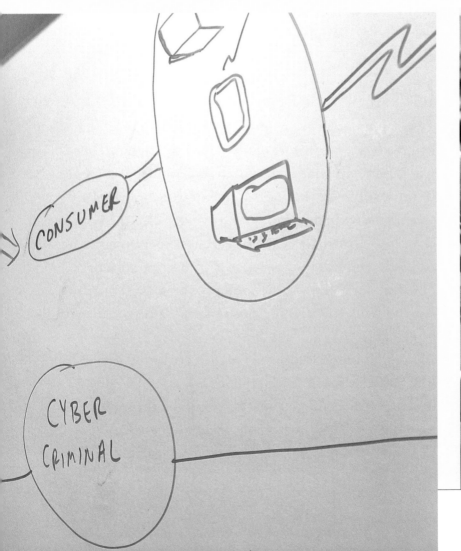

information regarding cybersecurity threats with the Department of Homeland Security. Businesses must work to keep their computer networks safe from outside attacks.

Simultaneously, the United Nations is meeting to discuss the international telecommunication treaty. Cybersecurity affects global commerce, online freedoms, and technological innovations. Since the Internet is not controlled by a government body or one private company, it will be difficult to regulate cyberspace.

IN THE FUTURE

Twenty-first-century technology presents many challenges to our constitutionally protected rights. There will be new legislation, regulations, and legal disputes. In our evolving cyberworld, the approaches to protecting individual rights are evolving. Since the courts have not construed "virtual searches" as Fourth Amendment searches because they do not require physical entry onto someone's property, the Fourth Amendment is becoming obsolete as a protected right of privacy.

Modern technology has made the need for warrants and reasonable searches and seizures irrelevant if most of the evidence can be obtained through alternate means. Therefore, some argue that the Supreme Court should require law enforcement to at least

WAR ON TERROR

The Constitution grants Congress the power to declare war as recommended by the president of the United States, as commander in chief. Traditionally, our country has gone to war against one or more sovereign nations. The "war" must be declared based on its own merits. However, as Professor Bruce Ackerman states in his book *Before the Next Attack: Preserving Civil Liberties in the Age of Terrorism*, a war on terrorism gives the president unilateral power to initiate "battle" against the enemy without congressional consent. Terrorism is a serious threat to our national security, but if it is viewed as a never-ending "war," then our civil liberties will be permanently impacted.

As the war on terror pertains to civil liberties, immigrants, especially with Muslim or Arab names, were subjected to detention and suspected of being terrorist operatives by the NSA, FBI, CIA, and Justice Department. According to the ACLU, after 9/11, government intelligence officials rifled through immigrants' computers, cell phones, and address books looking for connections to al-Qaeda operatives around the world. The rights of the Constitution must protect all Americans regardless of their country of origin, race, gender, or affiliations.

show that there is "reasonable suspicion" to use cameras to follow a specific individual or prove "probable cause" to search an individual's bank or telephone records. This would protect the rights of privacy

under the Fourth Amendment but allow law enforcement to use modern technology to aid its efforts to keep us safe.

With respect to the First Amendment, the Constitution states that freedom of speech must be protected even if the ideas and expressions are false, offensive, or hurtful. Ideas that are worthy of credibility and respect are those that hold up to criticism. For example, when the leaders of Iran claimed that the Holocaust did not happen, people responded by calling the remarks offensive to Jewish people. The fact is these remarks were false and historical evidence proves that the Holocaust did happen. The Holocaust deniers should be called out for their ignorance, not for being anti-Semitic. The Constitution cannot prevent people from offending others. The key to a free society is to allow the expression even if it will offend our values.

Both the First Amendment and the Fourth Amendment of the Bill of Rights are fundamental to our democratic society. They both involve personal rights of security and privacy. Digital technology is advancing faster than our government and civil rights groups can comprehend the effects on our Constitutional rights. The United States does not have jurisdiction or authority to regulate what is distributed on the Internet. Some countries have tried to censor individuals and corporations for the

The crafters of the Constitution could never have imagined a day when people would communicate through smartphones and social networks. This makes protecting the rights of individuals more challenging than ever before.

information they send on the Internet. No entity can control what is on the Internet since no one government, corporation, or organization controls the content provided on the Internet.

Privacy in the information age warrants that the government and private businesses protect citizens' personal information when it is collected on a database. We must demand the same protection of the privacy of our identities as we have historically required for our homes and personal papers. Our personal information should be considered our "property." Additional federal and state regulations are needed to protect individual's privacy.

One of the biggest problems we face today is that we are bombarded with information from numerous sources around the clock. Corruption of the public dialogue by ideological groups to distort the facts in our social and political conversation is at an all-time high. News media, online sources, and blog "experts" claim to distribute the facts.

Our Founding Fathers created the Constitution and the Bill of Rights so they could be adapted to an ever-changing world. They could not have imagined the invention of the television, Internet, satellite radio, or smartphones. New technology makes it difficult for lawmakers and our court system to keep up with how these advances affect our constitutionally protected rights.

Preamble to the Constitution

We the People of the United States, in order to form a more perfect Union, establish Justice, insure domestic Tranquility, provide for the common defense, promote the general Welfare, and secure the Blessings of Liberty to ourselves and our Posterity, do ordain and establish this Constitution for the United States of America.

On September 25, 1789, Congress transmitted to the state legislatures twelve proposed amendments, two of which, having to do with congressional representation and congressional pay, were not adopted. The remaining ten amendments became the Bill of Rights.

The Bill of Rights

Amendment I

Congress shall make no law respecting an establishment of religion, or prohibiting the free exercise thereof; or abridging the freedom of speech, or of the press; or the right of the people peaceably to assemble, and to petition the Government for a redress of grievances.

Amendment II

A well regulated Militia, being necessary to the security of a free State, the right of the people to keep and bear Arms, shall not be infringed.

Amendment III

No Soldier shall, in time of peace be quartered in any house, without the consent of the Owner, nor in time of war, but in a manner to be prescribed by law.

Amendment IV

The right of the people to be secure in their persons, houses, papers, and effects, against unreasonable searches and seizures, shall not be violated, and no Warrants shall issue, but upon probable cause, supported by Oath or affirmation, and particularly describing the place to be searched, and the persons or things to be seized.

Amendment V

No person shall be held to answer for a capital, or otherwise infamous crime, unless on a presentment or indictment of a Grand Jury, except in cases arising in the land or naval forces, or in the Militia, when in actual service in time of War or public danger; nor shall any person be subject for the same offence to be twice put in jeopardy of life or limb; nor shall be compelled in any criminal case to be a witness against himself, nor be deprived of life, liberty, or property, without due process of law; nor shall private property be taken for public use, without just compensation.

Amendment VI

In all criminal prosecutions, the accused shall enjoy the right to a speedy and public trial, by an impartial jury of the State and district wherein the crime shall have been committed, which district shall have been previously ascertained by law, and to be informed of the nature and cause of the accusation; to be confronted with the witnesses against him; to have compulsory process for obtaining witnesses in his favor, and to have the Assistance of Counsel for his defense.

Amendment VII

In Suits at common law, where the value in controversy shall exceed twenty dollars, the right of trial by jury shall be preserved, and no fact tried by a jury, shall be otherwise reexamined in any Court of the United States, than according to the rules of the common law.

Amendment VIII

Excessive bail shall not be required, nor excessive fines imposed, nor cruel and unusual punishments inflicted.

Amendment IX

The enumeration in the Constitution, of certain rights, shall not be construed to deny or disparage others retained by the people.

Amendment X

The powers not delegated to the United States by the Constitution, nor prohibited by it to the States, are reserved to the States respectively, or to the people.

GLOSSARY

ACLU The American Civil Liberties Union, a non-profit organization that seeks to protect individual rights and freedoms.

biometrics The use of science to identify humans by their unique traits and characteristics (e.g., fingerprints, voice patterns, etc.).

censorship The suppression of words, pictures, or other expressions because they offend someone based on moral, political, or religious grounds.

copyright The legal right given to the creator of an original work to prevent infringement for a certain length of time.

cyberbullying Repeated and intentional harm inflicted through the use of computers, cell phones, or other electronic devices.

cyberspace The electronic universe created by computer networks.

data mining The process of analyzing information and summarizing it by patterns and relationships.

defamation The act of causing injury to someone's reputation by slander or libel.

Federal Trade Commission The FTC is a federal agency regulating interstate trade and consumer protection.

gag order A court order banning reporters, attorneys, and others from discussing a case in a court of law before a decision has been rendered.

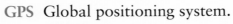

GPS Global positioning system.

Internet A worldwide network of computers communicating with each other.

Internet service provider (ISP) A company that charges you a monthly subscription fee to connect to the Internet.

libel A published false statement that is damaging to someone's reputation.

malice Intentional desire to do wrong.

malware Software that is intended to damage or disable computers and computer systems.

political correctness The avoidance, often considered as taken to extremes, of forms of expression or action that are perceived to exclude, marginalize, or insult groups of people who are socially disadvantaged or discriminated against.

probable cause Sufficient facts to establish that a crime has been committed or that evidence of a crime will probably be found in an area to be searched.

prurient Having or encouraging an excessive interest in sexual matters.

search warrant An official court order authorizing law enforcement to search a home or other property of someone suspected of committing a crime based on probable cause.

subpoena An order from a court for a person to appear at a trial under punishment for failure to appear.

surveillance Close and continuous observation, usually of a suspected criminal or spy.

USA Patriot Act United and Strengthening America by Providing Appropriate Tools Required to Intercept and Obstruct Terrorism Act of 2001.

WiFi A local area network that uses high frequency radio signals to transmit and receive data over distances.

Canadian Civil Liberties Association

506-360 Bloor Street West

Toronto, ON M5S 1X1

Canada

(416) 363-0321

Web site: http://www.ccla.org

The Canadian Civil Liberties Association is an organization dedicated to protecting the individual rights and liberties of its nation's citizens.

The Canadian Justice Review Board

Box 4853 Station E

Ottawa, Ontario K1S 5J1

Web site: http://www.canadianjusticereviewboard.ca

The Canadian Justice Review Board provides information about the Constitution of Canada, Canadian laws, and the rule of law in Canada.

The CATO Institute

1000 Massachusetts Ave. NW

Washington, DC 20001-5403

(202) 842-0200

Web site: http://www.cato.org

The CATO Institute is a public policy research organization.

Center for Democracy & Technology

1634 I Street NW #1100

Washington, DC 20006

(202) 637-9800

Web site: http://www.cdt.org
The Center for Democracy & Technology is a nonprofit public policy organization.

Center for Individual Freedom

917-B King Street

Alexandria, VA 22314

(703) 535-5836

Web site: http://www.cfif.org
The Center for Individual Freedom is a nonprofit organization with the mission to protect and defend individual freedoms and individual rights.

The Center for Internet Security

31 Tech Valley Drive, Suite 2

East Greenbush, NY 12061

(518) 226-3460

Web site: http://www.cisecurity.org
The Center for Internet Security is an organization designed to enhance the security readiness and response of public and private sector entities.

Electronic Privacy Information Center

1718 Connecticut Ave. NW, Suite 200

Washington, DC 20009

(202) 483-1140

Web site: http://www.epic.org
The Electronic Privacy Information Center is a public interest research center dedicated to protecting online privacy.

Goldwater Institute

500 E. Coronado Road

Phoenix, AZ 85004

(602) 462-5000

Web site: http://www.goldwaterinstitute.org

The Goldwater Institute is a nonprofit organization assisting states to promote individual liberties.

The House of Representatives

U.S. House of Representatives

Washington, DC 20515

(202) 224-3121

Web site: http://www.house.gov

The House of Representatives provides information how Congress and the other two branches of the government operate.

The National Archives

700 Pennsylvania Avenue, NW

Washington, DC 20408

(866) 272-6272

Web site: http://www.archives.gov

The National Archives provides the texts of the Declaration of Independence, the Constitution, and the Bill of Rights.

Public Knowledge

1818 N Street NW

Suite 410

Washington, DC 20036

(202) 861-0020

Web site: http://www.publicknowledge.org

Public Knowledge is an organization that promotes openness of the Internet.

The United Nations

1 United Nations Plaza

New York, New York 10017

(212) 963-1234

Web site: http://www.unrol.org

The United Nations provides information on efforts to develop the rule of law in countries around the world.

WEB SITES

Due to the changing nature of Internet links, Rosen Publishing has developed an online list of Web sites related to the subject of this book. This site is updated regularly. Please use this link to access the list:

http://www.rosenlinks.com/PFCD/Info

FOR FURTHER READING

Allen, James. *Individual Liberty*. Whitefish, MT: Kessinger Publishing, LLC, 2010.

Clarke, Richard A., and Robert K. Knake. *Cyber War: The Next Threat to National Security and What to Do About It*. New York, NY: HarperCollins Publishers, 2010.

Hinduja, Sameer, and Justin W. Patchin. *Bullying Beyond the Schoolyard: Preventing and Responding to Cyberbullying*. Thousand Oaks, CA: Crown Press, 2009.

Menn, Joseph. *Fatal System Error: The Hunt for the New Crime Lords Who Are Bringing Down the Internet*. New York, NY: PublicAffairs, 2010.

Mitnick, Kevin. *Ghost in the Wires: My Adventures as the World's Most Wanted Hacker*. New York, NY: Brown, 2011.

Paul, Ron. *Liberty Defined: 50 Essential Issues That Affect Our Freedom*. New York, NY: Grand Central Publishing, 2011.

Poulsen, Kevin. *Kingpin: How One Hacker Took Over the Billion-Dollar Cybercrime Underground*. New York, NY: Crown Publishing Group, 2011.

Ackerman, Bruce. *Before the Next Attack: Preserving Civil Liberties in an Age of Terror*. New Haven, CT: Yale University Press, 2006.

Alderman, Ellen, and Caroline Kennedy. *The Right to Privacy*. New York, NY: Alfred A. Knopf, Inc., 1995.

Andrews, Lori. *I Know Who You Are and I Saw What You Did: Social Networks and the Death of Privacy*. New York, NY: Free Press, 2011.

Brin, David. *The Transparent Society*. Reading, MA: Addison-Wesley, 1998.

Espejo, Roman. *Civil Liberties* (Opposing Viewpoints). Farmington Hills, MI: Greenhaven Press, 2009.

Garfinkel, Simson. *Database Nation: The Death of Privacy in the 21st Century*. Sebastopol, CA: O'Reilly & Associates, Inc., 2000.

Gertler, Eric J. *Prying Eyes: Protect Your Privacy from People Who Sell to You, Snoop On You, and Steal from You*. New York, NY: Random House, 2004.

Hentoff, Nat. *The War on the Bill of Rights and the Gathering Resistance*. New York, NY: Seven Stories Press, 2003.

Holtzman, David. *Privacy Lost: How Technology Is Endangering Your Privacy*. San Francisco, CA: Jossey-Bass Publishers, 2006.

Hunter, Richard. *World Without Secrets: Business, Crime, and Privacy in the Age of Ubiquitous*

BIBLIOGRAPHY

Computers. New York, NY: John Wiley & Sons, 2002.

Klinkner, Philip A. *The American Heritage History of the Bill of Rights: The First Amendment*. Englewood Cliffs, NJ: Silver Burdett Press, 1991.

Kuhn, Betsy. *Prying Eyes: Privacy in the Twenty-First Century*. Minneapolis, MN: Twenty-First Century Books, 2008.

Nissenbaum, Helen. *Privacy in Context: Technology, Privacy and the Integrity of Social Life*. Palo Alto, CA: Stanford University Press, 2010.

Nunziato, Dawn C. *Virtual Freedom: Net Neutrality and Free Speech in the Internet Age*. Palo Alto, CA: Stanford University Press, 2009.

Phillips, Christopher. *Constitution Café: Jefferson's Brew for a True Revolution*. New York, NY: W.W. Norton & Company, Inc., 2011.

Ratner, Michael, and Margaret Ratner Kunstler. *Hell No: Your Right to Dissent in Twenty-First Century America*. New York, NY: Center for Constitutional Rights, 2011.

Romero, Anthony D., and Dina Temple-Raston. *In Defense of Our America: The Fight for Civil Liberties in the Age of Terror*. New York, NY: HarperCollins, 2007.

Rothfeder, Jeffrey. *Privacy for Sale*. New York, NY: Simon & Schuster, 1992.

Solove, Daniel J., and Paul M. Schwartz. *Privacy, Information, and Technology*. New York, NY: Wolters Kluwer, 2011.

Williams, Juan. *Muzzled: The Assault on Honest Debate*. New York, NY: Crown Publishers, 2011.

Zeinert, Karen. *Free Speech: From Newspapers to Music Lyrics*. Springfield, NJ: Enslow Publishers, Inc., 1995.

A

About the Author

Suzanne Weinick graduated from the University at Albany, State University of New York, in 1986 with a bachelor's of arts degree, majoring in political science and minoring in communications. She went on to Hofstra University School of Law and practiced corporate law full-time until she became a mom. She now enjoys writing about constitutional liberties.

Photo Credits

Cover, pp. 1, 3, 4, 8, 28, 38–39, 44, 63, 66–67, 80 Bloomberg/Getty Images; pp. 5, 16–17, 24–25, 52–53, 58, 81, 86–87 © AP Images; p. 9 © Greg Mathieson/MAI/ Landov; pp. 10–11 Jewel Samad/AFP/Getty Images; pp. 22–23 SuperStock/Getty Images; p. 29 © Mario Anzuoni/Reuters/Landov; p. 32 Brendan O'Sullivan/ Photolibrary/Getty Images; pp. 36–37 © iStockphoto.com/ Phillip Bartlett; p. 45 Paul Morigi/Getty Images; pp. 48–49 AFP/Getty Images; pp. 64–65 © Virgin (UK)/ Everett Collection; pp. 70–71 Google/Connie Zhou/AP Images; p. 75 Dave Einsel/Getty Images; pp. 76–77 Justin Sullivan/ Getty Images; pp. 82–83 Karen Bleier/AFP/Getty Images; p. 91 iStockphoto/Thinkstock; page and text box border images © iStockphoto.com/Wayne Howard (crowd & flag), © iStockphoto.com/DHuss (U. S. Capitol building), © iStockphoto.com/Andrea Gingerich (faces).

Designer: Nicole Russo; Editor: Nicholas Croce; Photo Researcher: Amy Feinberg